P9-CFZ-446

DISCARD

◨ READERS

Level 2

Dinosaur Dinners
Fire Fighter!
Bugs! Bugs! Bugs!
Slinky, Scaly Snakes!
Animal Hospital
The Little Ballerina
Munching, Crunching, Sniffing,
    and Snooping
The Secret Life of Trees
Winking, Blinking, Wiggling,
    and Waggling
Astronaut: Living in Space
Twisters!
Holiday! Celebration Days
    around the World
The Story of Pocahontas
Horse Show
Survivors: The Night the Titanic Sank
Eruption! The Story of Volcanoes
The Story of Columbus
Journey of a Humpback Whale
Amazing Buildings
Feathers, Flippers, and Feet
Outback Adventure: Australian Vacation
Sniffles, Sneezes, Hiccups, and Coughs
Ice Skating Stars
Let's Go Riding

I Want to Be a Gymnast
Starry Sky
Earth Smart: How to Take Care
    of the Environment
Water Everywhere
Telling Time
A Trip to the Theater
Journey of a Pioneer
Inauguration Day
Star Wars: Journey Through Space
Star Wars: A Queen's Diary
Star Wars: R2-D2 and Friends
Star Wars: Jedi in Training
Star Wars Clone Wars: Anakin in Action!
Star Wars Clone Wars: Stand Aside – Bounty
    Hunters!
Star Wars: Join the Rebels
WWE: John Cena
Spider-Man: Worst Enemies
Power Rangers: Great Adventures
Pokémon: Meet the Pokémon
Pokémon: Meet Ash!
Meet the X-Men
Indiana Jones: Traps and Snares
¡Insectos! *en español*
¡Bomberos! *en español*
La Historia de Pocahontas *en español*

Level 3

Shark Attack!
Beastly Tales
Titanic
Invaders from Outer Space
Movie Magic
Time Traveler
Bermuda Triangle
Tiger Tales
Plants Bite Back!
Zeppelin: The Age of the Airship
Spies
Terror on the Amazon
Disasters at Sea
The Story of Anne Frank
Abraham Lincoln: Lawyer, Leader, Legend
George Washington: Soldier, Hero, President
Extreme Sports
Spiders' Secrets
The Big Dinosaur Dig
Space Heroes: Amazing Astronauts
The Story of Chocolate
School Days Around the World
Polar Bear Alert!
Welcome to China
My First Ballet Show
Ape Adventures

Greek Myths
Amazing Animal Journeys
Spacebusters: The Race to the Moon
WWE: Triple H
WWE: Undertaker
Star Wars: Star Pilot
Star Wars: I Want to Be a Jedi
Star Wars: The Story of Darth Vader
Star Wars: Yoda in Action
Star Wars: Forces of Darkness
Star Wars: Death Star Battles
Marvel Heroes: Amazing Powers
The X-Men School
Pokémon: Explore with Ash and Dawn
Pokémon: Become a Pokémon Trainer
The Invincible Iron Man: Friends and
    Enemies
Wolverine: Awesome Powers
Abraham Lincoln: Abogado, Líder, Leyenda
    en español
Al Espacio: La Carrera a la Luna
    en español
Fantastic Four: The World's Greatest
    Superteam
Fantastic Four: Adversaries

A Note to Parents

DK READERS is a compelling program for beginning readers, designed in conjunction with leading literacy experts, including Dr. Linda Gambrell, Distinguished Professor of Education at Clemson University. Dr. Gambrell has served as President of the National Reading Conference, the College Reading Association, and the International Reading Association.

Beautiful illustrations and superb full-color photographs combine with engaging, easy-to-read stories to offer a fresh approach to each subject in the series. Each DK READER is guaranteed to capture a child's interest while developing his or her reading skills, general knowledge, and love of reading.

The five levels of DK READERS are aimed at different reading abilities, enabling you to choose the books that are exactly right for your child:

Pre-level 1: Learning to read
Level 1: Beginning to read
Level 2: Beginning to read alone
Level 3: Reading alone
Level 4: Proficient readers

The "normal" age at which a child begins to read can be anywhere from three to eight years old. Adult participation through the lower levels is very helpful for providing encouragement, discussing storylines, and sounding out unfamiliar words.

No matter which level you select, you can be sure that you are helping your child learn to read, then read to learn!

LONDON, NEW YORK, MUNICH,
MELBOURNE, AND DELHI

Project Editor Shaila Awan
Art Editor Susan Calver
US Editor Regina Kahney
Production Editor Marc Staples
Picture Researcher Martin Redfern
Jacket Designer Natalie Godwin
Publishing Manager Bridget Giles
Art Director Martin Wilson
Natural History Consultant
Theresa Greenaway

Reading Consultant
Linda B. Gambrell, Ph.D.

First American Edition, 1998
This edition, 2011
11 12 13 14 15 16 10 9 8 7 6 5 4 3 2 1
Published in the United States by DK Publishing
375 Hudson Street, New York, New York 10014

Published in Great Britain by Dorling Kindersley Limited.

DK books are available at special discounts when purchased in bulk
for sales promotions, premiums, fund-raising, or educational use.
For details, contact: DK Publishing Special Markets
375 Hudson Street, New York, New York 10014
SpecialSales@dk.com

A catalog record for this book is available
from the Library of Congress

ISBN: 978-0-7566-7205-8 (pb)
ISBN: 978-0-7566-7206-5 (plc)

Color reproduction by Colourscan, Singapore
Printed and bound in China by L Rex Printing Co., Ltd.

The publisher would like to thank the following for their kind permission to
reproduce their photographs: Key: t=top, b=below, l=left, r=right, c=center
Biofotos: C. Andrew Henley 14–15; **Bruce Coleman:** Gerald Cubitt 24br;
M.P.L. Fogden 9bl; Peter Zabransky 17tr; **FLPA:** Larry West 23br; **NHPA:**
Stephen Dalton 12–13, 27tr; OSF: G.I. Bernard 29br; J.A.L. Cooke 15tr; **Planet
Earth Pictures:** Brian Kenney 26–27; **Warren Photographic:** Kim Taylor 13cr.
Jacket images: *Front:* **Alamy Images:** Arco Images GmbH / Meul, J.
Warren Photographic: Kim Taylor tc.
Additional photography by Jane Burton, Neil Fletcher, Frank Greenaway,
Colin Keates, Harry Taylor, Kim Taylor, Jerry Young

All other images © Dorling Kindersley.
For further information see www.dkimages.com

Discover more at

www.dk.com

DK READERS

BEGINNING TO READ ALONE 2

Bugs Bugs Bugs!

Written by Jennifer Dussling

DK Publishing

Stag beetle

Yikes!
Bugs look scary close up.
But <u>you</u> don't need to worry.

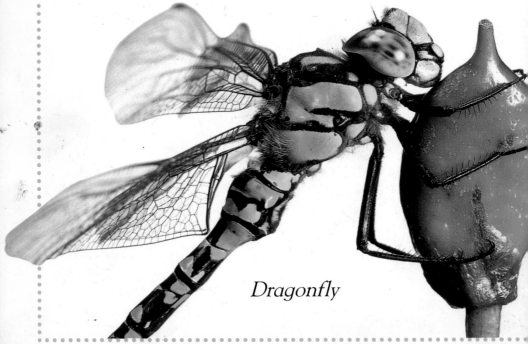

Dragonfly

Most bugs are a danger only to other insects. They are the bugs that really bug other bugs.

Praying mantis

Beetle-hunting wasp

5

This praying mantis
sits perfectly still.
But if you are a bug,
watch out!
A fly lands on a branch
near a praying mantis.
The mantis fixes its
big eyes on the fly.

In a second,
the mantis lashes out.
Its front legs trap the fly.
They pull it to the mantis's mouth.
Munch, crunch—
soon the fly is gone!

Some bugs hunt other bugs,
not to eat themselves,
but to feed to their babies.
This hunting wasp
has just stung a beetle.

It will drag the beetle to its nest
and lay eggs on the beetle.
When the eggs hatch,
the young wasps, called grubs,
will eat the beetle up.

Hairy food

One kind of wasp
catches huge spiders
for its grubs.
It sometimes takes over
the spider's home, too!

Wood ants are tiny.
But they have sharp jaws
and they can squirt acid
from their bodies.
This acid can kill
another bug.

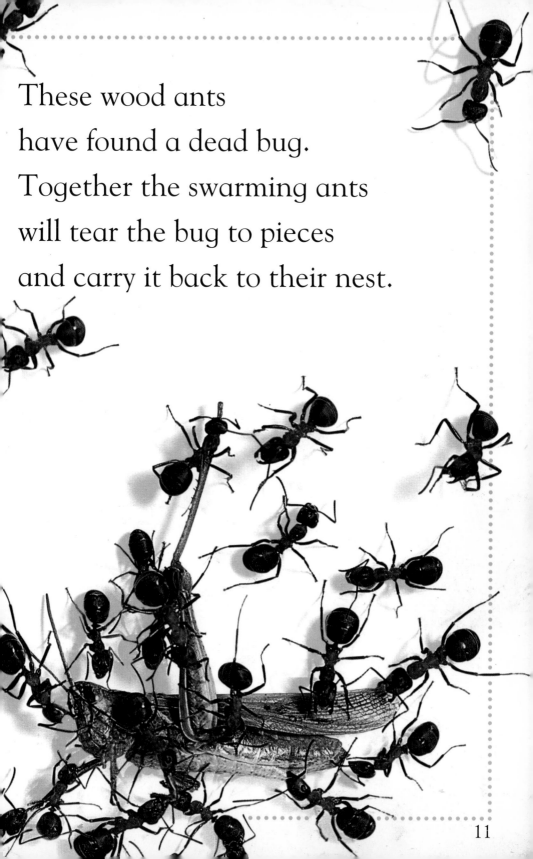

These wood ants
have found a dead bug.
Together the swarming ants
will tear the bug to pieces
and carry it back to their nest.

It is a quiet day by a pond.
One second, a mosquito
is buzzing along.
The next second,
a dragonfly swoops down
and snaps the mosquito
right out of the air!

Dragonflies are flying killers
that eat and eat and eat.
In half an hour, they can eat
their own body weight.
That's like you eating
250 hot dogs!

Ancient insect
Dragonflies were around
long before the dinosaurs!
This dragonfly rotted away
millions of years ago.
It left its print in a rock.

An assassin is a person who kills another person on purpose. The assassin bug is a bug that really lives up to its name.

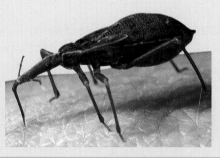

When it catches another insect,
it injects the insect with poison.

The poison turns
the bug's insides to soup.
Then the assassin bug
sucks up the soup!

Only one bug
has to watch out for
a male stag beetle—
another male stag beetle!
What do they fight about?
Usually a female
stag beetle!

Short, sharp jaws

A female stag beetle
has smaller jaws
than a male.
But she can give
a much sharper bite.

The fighting beetles
poke at each other,
then lock jaws.

One beetle grabs
the other beetle
and throws him.
The loser
scurries away.

Monarch butterfly caterpillar

With so many killer bugs
and other hungry animals,
how do any insects survive?

Hoverfly

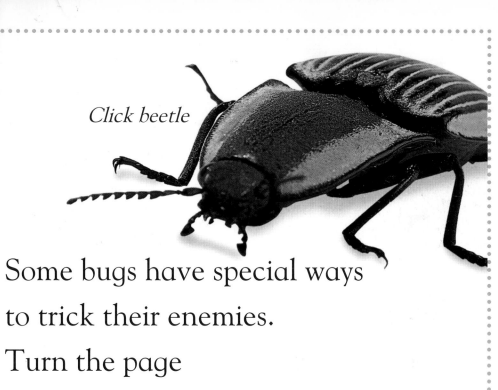

Click beetle

Some bugs have special ways
to trick their enemies.
Turn the page
and read all about them!

*Postman
butterfly
caterpillar*

Stinkbugs have glands
that make smells.
Some stinkbugs
ooze a nasty-smelling liquid
when they are in danger.
That's a big turnoff!

Stinkbugs are also known
as shield bugs.
Some use their flat bodies
to shield their young
from hungry insects and birds.

The monarch butterfly
looks easy to capture and eat.
But hungry bugs and birds
leave it alone.
Why?

In the insect world,
bright colors are a warning.
Bright orange signals that
this butterfly tastes bad.
Even the monarch caterpillars
taste awful.

Changing faces

When a caterpillar
is fully grown,
it changes into a butterfly
inside a hard case like this,
called a chrysalis (KRISS-uh-liss).

Tropical lappet moth caterpillar

This caterpillar's long hairs break easily.
When enemies try to catch it, they get a mouthful of hair instead!

Safety in numbers
Caterpillars sometimes huddle together.
They flick their heads up to startle a hungry enemy.

And this spiky caterpillar
can be deadly.
The leaves that it eats
make its body poisonous.
It is not harmed by the poison,
but its enemies are!

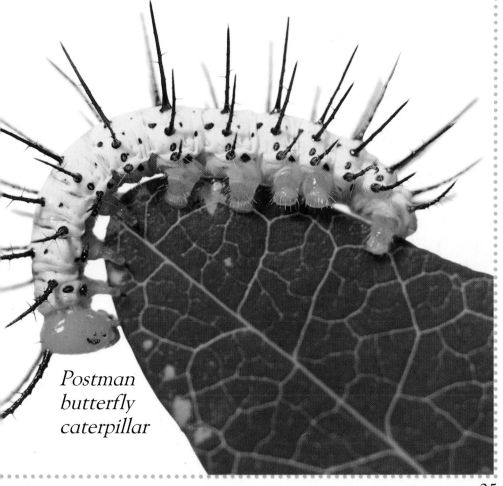

*Postman
butterfly
caterpillar*

A thorn bug is good at hiding.
It looks like a thorn on a twig.
A bird looking for a meal
might not see it.

Thorn bugs are smart, too.
They sometimes all face
the same way
and stay very still!

To avoid being eaten,
this click beetle
has a clever way of escaping.

It arches its back and then
jumps into the air.

If the beetle
lands upside-down,
it throws itself into the air again—
this time hoping to land safely
on its feet!

Flashing lights

Some click beetles send out light signals. These flashing lights help the beetles to find a mate.

One of these bugs
is a harmless hoverfly.
The other is a hornet
with a nasty sting.
Can you tell
which is which?
No?

Neither can most bugs and birds!
That's why they leave
both of these insects alone.
Still don't know which is which?
The fly is the bug
on the left!

Bug facts

There are at least one million
different kinds of insects
in the world.

Sometimes all insects
are called "bugs."
But the true bugs are those
that have sharp,
strawlike tubes for feeding.

All insects have six legs,
and most have wings
at some time in their lives.

Some insects hear with their legs.
Other insects taste with their feet.

A few insects eat and eat
when they are young.
But when they get older,
they don't eat anything at all.

Some bugs have amazing vision
and can see colors
that people cannot see.

Index